‹SURINAME›

MAJOR WORLD NATIONS

SURINAME

Noëlle B. Beatty

CHELSEA HOUSE PUBLISHERS
Philadelphia

Chelsea House Publishers

Contributing Author: Jeff Beneke

Copyright © 1999 by Chelsea House Publishers,
a division of Main Line Book Co.
All rights reserved.
Printed and bound in the United States of America.

3 5 7 9 8 6 4 2

Library of Congress Cataloging-in-Publication Data

Beatty, Noelle B.
Suriname / Noëlle B. Beatty.
p.   cm.
Includes index.
Summary: An overview of the history, geography, economy, government,
people, and culture of the country on the northeast coast
of South America formerly known as Dutch Guiana.
ISBN 0–7910–4748–2 (hardcover)
1. Surinam—Juvenile literature.   [1. Surinam.]
I. Title.
F2408.5.B43   1997
988.3—dc21   97–17786
CIP
AC

◄ C O N T E N T S ►

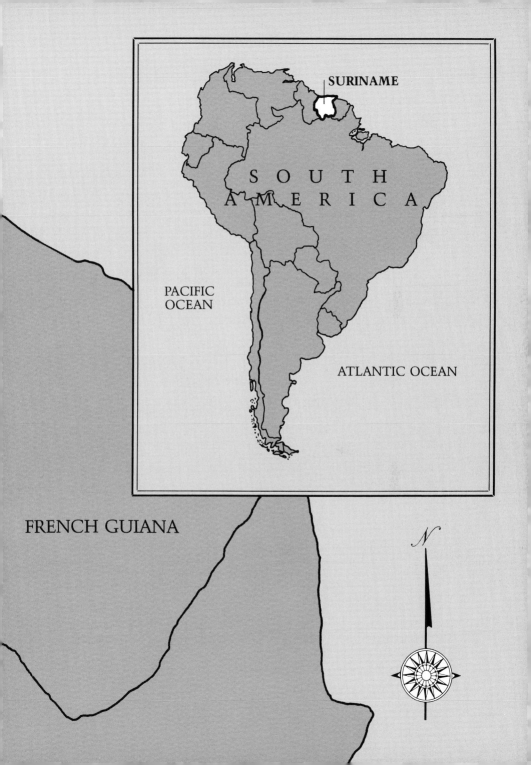

SURINAME

SOUTH AMERICA

PACIFIC
OCEAN

ATLANTIC OCEAN

FRENCH GUIANA

N

◄ FACTS AT A GLANCE ►

Land and People

Area	63,037 square miles (163,896 square kilometers)
Highest Point	Juliana Top, 4,120 feet (1,236 meters)
Coastline	215 miles (346 kilometers)
Major Rivers	Suriname, Tapanahoni, Saramacca, Coppename, Nickerie, Commerwijne, Corantijn
Capital	Paramaribo (population 200,970)
Other Major Cities	Nieuw Nickerie, Meerzorg, Marienburg
Average Annual Rainfall	80 inches (2,032 millimeters), coastal; 60 inches (1,524 millimeters), inland
Population	436,418
Population Density	6.9 people per square mile (2.7 per sq km)
Population Distribution	Rural, 51 percent; urban, 49 percent
Official Language	Dutch
Other Languages	English, Hindi, Javanese, Chinese, Sranan Tongo
Literacy Rate	93 percent
Major Ethnic Groups	Hindus, Creoles, Indonesians, Maroons, Indians, Chinese, Europeans, and Middle Easterners
Religions	Hindu, 27 percent; Roman Catholic, 23 percent; Muslim, 20 percent; Protestant, 25 percent
Infant Mortality Rate	30 per 1,000 live births
Average Life Expectancy	70 years (males, 67.5 years; females, 72.7 years)

Economy

Major Resources	Bauxite, iron ore, lumber, gold, fish, shrimp
Major Exports	Alumina and aluminum (85 percent of export income), fish and shrimp, rice, bananas
Export Partners	Norway (33 percent), Netherlands (26 percent), United States (13 percent), Japan (6 percent), Brazil (6 percent)
Major Imports	Machinery and transport equipment, fuels and lubricants, foodstuffs, cotton
Import Partners	United States (42 percent), Netherlands (22 percent), Trinidad and Tobago (10 percent), Brazil (5 percent)
Major Crops	Rice, coffee, cacao, coconuts, bananas, peanuts, citrus fruits, sugarcane
Currency	Suriname guilder (also called florin), divided into 100 cents

Government

Form of Government	Republic
Executive Branch	President and prime minister, elected for 5-year terms by the National Assembly; Cabinet of Ministers appointed by the president from members of the National Assembly
Legislative Branch	National Assembly (51 members)
Judicial Branch	Supreme Court, justices nominated for life

◄HISTORY AT A GLANCE►

by 2000 B.C.	American Indians have discovered agriculture, pottery, and weaving. The Arawak and the Carib are the main tribes of Guiana.
by 1400 A.D.	The Caribs have almost wiped out the Arawaks. The Caribs maintain sea trade along the Guiana coast.
1498	On his third voyage to the New World, Christopher Columbus sights the Guiana coast.
1499	Amerigo Vespucci, an Italian navigator sailing for Spain, lands on Guiana and claims it for Spain.
1500s	The Netherlands, England, and France send expeditions along the coast but do not land.
by the early 1600s	Spain has given up hope of finding large deposits of gold in Guiana and ignores its claim to the territory.
1621	The Dutch establish a small trading settlement.
1620 to 1640	The English and French also develop small settlements.
1651	English settlers from the Caribbean island of Barbados set up the first long-lasting colony. Within a few years, they have started 500 sugarcane plantations and have brought in African slaves to work them.
1665 to 1674	England and the Netherlands go to war twice in Europe. The conflict extends to the New World.
1667	The Dutch conquer the English colony in Guiana. The Treaty of Breda allows the Dutch to keep the colony in return for giving their New Amsterdam colony to the English.

1686	Dutch settlers and native Indians sign a peace treaty, but Indian raids on plantations continue.
1759	A black slave named Kwaku leads a revolt against the plantation owners.
1760	A treaty allows Kwaku and other rebellious slaves to settle in the interior.
1796 to 1814	England and the Netherlands clash again. England captures and controls Dutch Guiana.
1815	The Treaty of Vienna restores the colony to the Dutch.
1863	The Dutch abolish slavery.
1866	Some residents are permitted to vote for members of a local parliament.
late 1800s	The Dutch import many Asians to work on the plantations. Chinese, Indians, and Javanese become part of the colony's ethnic mix.
1917	World War I stimulates interest in new sources of aluminum. Bauxite mining begins in the colony.
1922	Dutch Guiana ships its first bauxite ore.
1949	All residents are allowed to participate in politics.
1954	The local parliament and prime minister gain control of internal affairs. The Netherlands remains responsible for foreign relations.
1973	A Creole named Henck Arron is elected prime minister. He vows to make Dutch Guiana independent.
1975	Dutch Guiana becomes the independent republic of Suriname.
1975 to 1980	The market for bauxite falls. One-third of the population emigrates to the Netherlands.
1980	The army overthrows the civilian government. The elected National Assembly is replaced with a National Military Council. An officer named Desire Bouterse

takes the title of commander and controls the army and the government.

1982　Bouterse survives several unsuccessful attempts to overthrow his regime.

1984　Bouterse appoints a Supreme Council to control all governmental and military matters. He continues to rule the country as commander.

1986　Guerrilla war breaks out, disrupting the economy.

1987　New constitution restores civilian government, establishes a 51-member National Assembly with the power to select a president.

1988　Ramsewak Shankar elected president by the National Assembly.

1990　Military forces the resignations of the president and vice president.

1991　New National Assembly elected. Ronald Venetiaan becomes president.

1992　Government signs peace treaty with Maroon and Amerindian insurgents.

1996　Jules Wijdenbosch elected president by a People's Assembly.

The Government Square in the capital, Paramaribo, is peaceful today, but it has been the scene of violence in the years since Suriname won its independence.

Suriname and the World

Suriname, on the northern Atlantic coast of South America, is one of the newer independent countries of the world. Until 1975, it was the colony of Dutch Guiana, a possession of the Netherlands.

Like many of the nations that have become independent since the end of World War II, Suriname is a country whose identity is not yet firmly established. The first few years after independence were tranquil ones, but the country has since been troubled by recurring economic and political difficulties.

For most of its history, the land that today is Suriname has been remarkable among South American countries for the harmony among its many different peoples. American Indians, Africans, East Indians, Javanese, Chinese, Europeans, and Middle Easterners have lived together with little friction between groups or individuals. Under Dutch rule, the country came to enjoy one of the highest standards of living of any developing nation, which further promoted harmony.

Until the abolition of slavery in the mid-19th century, the European owners of Dutch Guiana's highly productive sugar plantations held most of the country's wealth. But as sugar's importance declined in the early 20th century, another source of wealth appeared. This was bauxite, the material from which aluminum is refined. Rich deposits of this mineral in the interior of Dutch Guiana attracted international investors and kept the country's balance of trade favorable—it exported more than it imported. Employment in the bauxite mines and processing plants supported the growth of other industries and spread the wealth among people far from the interior.

Conditions continued to be generally good for the first five years after Suriname achieved independence in 1975. The Netherlands continued to support its former colony with generous annual grants, and the United States also supplied aid. When world demand for aluminum dropped sharply in the late 1970s, the aid money helped cushion Suriname's economy. And the country's thriving agricultural and fishing industries provided food for the people and products to export abroad.

But a few signs of trouble had already begun to appear. In the first few years after independence, many well-educated businessmen, professionals, and teachers chose to leave Suriname for the Netherlands, where they felt their futures would be more secure. Industries, schools, and other major operations that were now short of highly skilled personnel ran less efficiently, either bringing in less revenue or operating at a loss. A teacher shortage meant that fewer students were prepared to enter the university or to take management jobs in business, and the nation's once-high literacy rate declined.

With the help of foreign loans, Suriname built a dam to provide hydroelectric power.

In these areas, Suriname's "growing pains" resembled those of other newly independent nations. But the country's situation became dramatically worse after a 1980 military coup overthrew its constitutional civilian government. The United States, the Netherlands, other European countries, and some of Suriname's South American neighbors watched with concern, and international companies became less willing to invest there. After the military government rounded up and executed a group of political opponents without trial in 1982, both the United States and the Netherlands protested by cutting off their aid.

Suriname remained under military rule for five more years, although opposition surfaced frequently. In 1987, civilian government finally returned, with the aid of a new constitution. Though the civilian president was overthrown by the military in 1990, new elections were soon held. Since installing the freely elected National Assembly in 1991, the government has made efforts to consolidate democracy and civilian rule.

Currently the outlook seems better for Suriname, though the political situation and the economy remain far from stable. If democratic rule continues, foreign countries will become more willing to invest in developing Suriname's rich natural resources. Because the diverse people of Suriname have traditionally been both resourceful and harmonious, many observers have strong hopes for the young nation.

Hills and mountains covered with thick forest make up 75 percent of Suriname's land area. In fact, only 3 percent of the land is inhabited or cultivated.

Tropical Country

The country of Suriname lies on the northeastern coast of South America, in a vast region known since earliest times as Guiana—"land surrounded by water" in the language of the local Indians. The region also includes the modern countries of Guyana, French Guiana, and parts of Venezuela and Brazil. Suriname's northern boundary stretches along the Atlantic Ocean for 215 miles (346 kilometers) between Guyana to the west and French Guiana to the east. About 300 miles (483 km) to the south, the country shares a border with Brazil. Slightly larger than the American state of Georgia, Suriname has an area of 63,037 square miles (163,896 square kilometers).

Suriname's neighbors dispute some of its borders. In the west, both Guyana and Suriname claim about 6,800 square miles (17,680 square kilometers) of borderland. French Guiana disputes the boundary of a small amount of territory in the southeast.

Suriname's location just above the equator gives the country a year-round tropical climate. Temperatures range from 70° Fahrenheit (21° Centigrade) to 90° F (32° C). The northeast trade winds bring breezes to the northern coastal plain and rain everywhere—especially to the interior.

Although a large amount of rain falls during the two rainy seasons, from April to August and from November to February, there is plenty of sunshine all year round. The average annual rainfall on the coast is 90 inches (2,286 millimeters). Despite the heavy rainfall and high humidity, Suriname has a generally healthful climate.

Suriname is divided into three distinct geographical zones: a narrow coastal plain in the north, a tropical forest and grassland area in the center, and a large region of heavily forested hills and low mountains extending to the Brazilian border in the south. Each of these zones forms a belt running east to west, parallel to the coast, all the way across the country.

The northern coastal zone, along the Atlantic Ocean, ranges from about 10 miles (16 kilometers) wide at the Marowijne River, which forms Suriname's eastern border with French Guiana, to 50 miles (81 km) wide at the Corantijn River, on the western border with Guyana. This small strip of land supports all of the country's cities, towns, and plantations and is home to 90 percent of the population.

South of this settled agricultural area lies the second zone, a band about 30 to 40 miles (48 to 64 kilometers) wide. This region includes a forest of low-growing shrubs and trees, broken occasionally by tropical grasslands, or savannas. Because the soil is sandy and infertile, attempts to grow crops in the area have been unsuccessful.

The low, rolling hills of the central zone are productive in one important way, however. They are the source of extensive deposits of bauxite, an ore that is manufactured into aluminum. The discovery of bauxite in this previously unproductive region brought about significant changes in the economy of Suriname.

Because the aluminum industry demands a great amount of electricity, a huge dam and hydroelectric power station have been constructed at Afobaka on the Suriname River to generate electricity. The dam has created the 600-square-mile (1,560-square-kilometer) Van Blommestein Lake, one of the largest artificial lakes in the world. The country has many potential hydroelectric sources because of its numerous large rivers. In addition to the Suriname, they include the Tapanahoni, in the southeast; the Saramacca, in the central region; the Coppename and Nickerie, which originate in the highlands of the northwest; and the Commewijne and Cottica in the northeast.

Suriname's third geographical zone, a thick rain forest, makes up about 75 percent of the country's area. This enormous rain forest is linked to the Amazon River Basin in northeastern Brazil. The Tumuc-Humac Mountains on the Brazilian border form the watershed of the Amazon River. All the rivers that flow into Suriname out of these hills eventually empty into the Atlantic Ocean.

The region's densely forested hills rise gradually into the Wilhelmina Mountains. There, Juliana Top peaks at about 4,120 feet (1,236 meters), the highest point in Suriname. There are no roads or densely populated settlements in this area, only rivers and mountains and small tribes of American Indians and descendants of African slaves who have lived here for hundreds of years.

However, the rain forest is far from empty: it is the natural habitat of unusual amphibians, poisonous reptiles, about 150 species of mammals, and more than 600 species of birds. Some of them are found only in this relatively small area of South America. One of these, the Surinam toad, bears the name of its native country (as it used to be spelled). A strong swimmer, the Surinam toad eats anything it can find in the fast-flowing rivers and streams in which it lives.

Another water-dweller, the Matamata turtle, may be the strangest-looking turtle in the world. Out of its rough and ridged carapace, or protective shell, protrudes a head that is completely flat and triangular in shape. This turtle lives mainly at the bottom of barely moving rivers and rests so long and so quietly that algae grow on its shell, making it difficult to see. When an unsuspecting fish swims by, the turtle opens its wide mouth and sucks in both water and the fish. Then it expels the water through a slit and swallows the fish whole.

Like the Matamata turtle, the caiman is a marine reptile that lives in slow, still waters. There are many species of caimans, all of which resemble crocodiles and inspire awe and terror. An early explorer in Guiana,

English naturalist Charles Waterton, described his "encounter with a cayman, the crocodile of tropical America," in his travel diary, *Journeys 1812– 1820 into Interior of Guiana*. With the help of the Indians with whom he was traveling, Waterton jumped on the caiman's back, killed it, and then examined it. He described the reptile, which no European had ever before seen: "The cayman's . . . teeth are entirely made for snatch and swallow. . . . Perhaps no animal in existence bears more decided marks in his countenance of cruelty and malice than the cayman. He is the scourge and terror of all the large rivers in South America near the line [equator]."

Also lurking in the rivers are piranha—small but vicious and sharp-toothed fish that can tear flesh into ribbons—and anacondas that can grow to more than 29 feet (9 meters) long. Relatives of the boa constrictor, these snakes kill their victims by squeezing them so hard they can no longer breathe. One of the world's most dangerous snakes, the bushmaster, is found only in the rain forest of Guiana and nearby countries. A rare and extremely deadly viper, the bushmaster has such a large supply of poison and such huge fangs that it can kill and eat a mammal the size of a small deer.

Another forest-dweller that lives near the water is the capybara, the world's largest rodent. A member of the mouse family, the capybara looks a little like a guinea pig—except that it grows to be 3 or 4 feet (about 1 meter) tall. Males and females look exactly alike, with large heads and square jaws. A plant-eating animal, the capybara has feet that are partly webbed like a duck's. These keep it firmly balanced in the water as it feeds on the thick vegetation in swampy marshes and at the edge of rivers.

Birds are the crowning glory of the rain forest. Hundreds of species of birds, most of them brightly colored, dart among the trees and *lianas* (woody vines that send their roots into the ground). Songbirds, green parrots, and colorful macaws call from the branches and are sometimes captured and kept as pets or sold by Indians. The male spangled cotinga boasts a plumage of shiny blue feathers. The Guianan cock-of-the-rock, another member of this brightly colored family, is about the size of a

Exotic birds, including the brightly colored cock-of-the-rock, inhabit the rain forest.

pigeon. It was given its name because the female makes her nest in protected breaks in rocks and the male has a comb (and a feisty temperament) similar to that of a rooster, or cock. The plumage of the mature male, including its comb, is an unforgettable brilliant orange.

The physical characteristics of Suriname have had a great influence on its economic and historical development. Most of the country is covered with vegetation so dense that no roads have been built, and only small settlements have been established. Only 3 percent of the total area—the flat plain along the Atlantic coast—is suitable for farming, settlements, and commerce. Because almost all Surinamese live on the coast, they have traditionally traded with Caribbean countries and with Europe much more frequently than with other countries on the South American continent.

Suriname's native inhabitants, the Arawak Indians, were conquered by the Caribs before the Europeans arrived. Today, only a few Arawak villages remain.

History

More than 10,000 years before the arrival of European explorers, the Arawak Indians of Guiana hunted prehistoric animals. As the mammoth and the mastodon gradually became extinct, the Indians relied more on the wild berries, fruits, and roots that grew on the fertile land. The coastal tribes lived by trapping fish and gathering shellfish.

Archaeologists studying Indian settlements dating from 2000 B.C. have discovered that the Arawaks cleared patches of ground and grew corn and root vegetables. They moved their villages when the ground was no longer fertile. In each new village, they built a large hut that served as a meeting and ceremonial space. They made pottery from local clay, learned to spin and weave cloth from cotton that grew wild on the coast, and became proficient boat builders.

The Arawak, Carib, and other Indian tribes of Guiana were also native to the West Indies—the chain of islands that stretches from Florida to the coast of Venezuela, separating the Atlantic Ocean from the Caribbean. In search of new lands, they voyaged over the sea between the islands of the West Indies and the northern coast of South America. Even before the first Europeans sailed to the West Indies in the 1400s, the fierce Caribs had driven most of the Arawak farmers from the islands. They had also driven out the Surinen, the Indian tribe that gave Suriname its name.

The Caribs were determined to claim new lands and they had the skills to do so. Excellent navigators, they understood river travel and were also able to guide 50-man canoes over long distances at sea. After conquering the Arawaks, they used their oceangoing skills to trade agricultural products, gold, and slaves with other Indian settlements.

The Caribs welcomed the first European explorers with gifts, but fought back when settlers arrived and began overrunning their lands and forcing their people into slavery. The Caribs' bows and arrows proved to be no match for the white men's guns and other, less obvious enemies. Entire villages were either conquered by the settlers or wiped out by smallpox and measles, diseases the newcomers brought from Europe. In the 1600s, the Indians of Suriname retreated into the interior rain forest, defeated by the adventurous Europeans who had come to the New World looking for land and fortune.

Exploration and Colonization

When Christopher Columbus made his third voyage to the New World, he sailed farther south than ever before. In 1498, he sailed along the coast of Guiana, all the way to the mouth of the Orinoco River in Venezuela. A year later, another Italian in the service of Spain, Amerigo Vespucci, landed on the coast of Guiana. Although the explorers claimed the region for Spain, they did not attempt to establish settlements. They were interested only in finding gold to send back to Spain.

By the early 1600s, the Spanish had lost interest in Guiana. They had given up hope of finding gold there and established productive colonies in other areas of South and Central America. At the same time, the Netherlands, Great Britain, and France began to see the potential profit to be made from colonizing South America. All three countries sought coastal sites that Spain had rejected, where they could grow sugar, coffee, rice, tobacco, and cotton to ship home to Europe. In 1621, the Dutch established a small settlement in Guiana. Between 1620 and 1640, the British and French also maintained small outposts there.

Columbus sailed along the Guianan coast in 1498 and claimed the region for Spain.

In 1651, the first full-fledged, successful colony was established in the region of central Guiana known today as Suriname. Its founders were a well-supplied band of English farmers who had set sail from the island of Barbados in the West Indies to settle a new plantation. The British colony prospered on the fertile coastal plain and produced cotton, coffee, and, most of all, sugar. The colonists also cultivated the cacao tree and learned from the Indians how to make cocoa and chocolate, new and highly admired products in Europe. In just a few years, the British established more than 500 small sugar plantations. They enlarged their colony by welcoming a number of Portuguese Jews who had fled from religious persecution in Brazil. This band of skilled laborers and businessmen with money to invest in plantation farming added to the stability of the colony.

For the most part, the successful growth of the plantations came about because of the forced labor of black slaves from Africa. The British brought about 2,000 slaves to the colony, which had a white population of only 1,000. Soon, British sailing vessels were supplying all of Guiana and the Caribbean area with African slaves. The colonists had also tried to force Indians to work on the plantations, but many of them died from the strenuous physical labor and from disease.

Over the next 150 years, from 1665 to 1815, European powers struggled against each other for control of the colonies in Guiana and elsewhere. From 1665 to 1674, the English and the Dutch fought two wars: one at home and one abroad. In 1667, the Dutch conquered the thriving British colony on the coast of central Guiana. In North America, the British captured the Dutch colony of Nieuw Amsterdam on the island of Manhattan and renamed it New York.

Under the Treaty of Breda, which ended the Anglo-Dutch Wars later in 1667, the two countries agreed to keep the territories they had just conquered. The Dutch were pleased with the arrangement because they wanted a tropical colony. They viewed their newly acquired territory as a paradise where their settlers could grow warm-weather crops to send home.

Dutch farmers took over the plantations and hired British ships to bring more slaves from Africa. Experienced at developing coastal plains in their own low-lying country, they expanded the available farmland by creating *polders*—areas of low land reclaimed from the sea. To hold back the flow of rainwater, the Dutch built dikes at the mouths of the Suriname and Saramacca rivers near the capital of Paramaribo, and at the Coppename and Nickerie rivers to the west. To control the tides, they constructed seawalls with floodgates on the ocean side of the new land. For irrigation and drainage, they dug canals. The soil reclaimed by the polders had a large concentration of clay but was still quite fertile. Sugarcane grown on this land soon was selling for high prices, making plantation farming a profitable way of life. By the late 18th century, the Dutch settlers were exporting more than 15 million pounds (6.8 million kilograms) of sugar, 18,000 lbs (8,100 kg) of coffee, 600,000 lbs (270,000 kg) of cocoa, and 160,000 lbs (72,000 kg) of cotton. More than 10,000 slaves worked in the agricultural fields and processing centers, supervised by a white population of about 1,500.

Even though the Treaty of Breda had settled the Anglo-Dutch Wars, the Dutch colony in Guiana was rarely at peace during the period that followed. The Indians who had lost their land to the Europeans repeatedly raided the plantations, even after they signed a peace treaty in 1686. French pirates several times attacked some of the smaller settlements, disrupting plantation life. These disturbances gave many slaves the opportunity to escape into the forest interior and led others to revolt.

The Dutch rulers sent expeditions into the interior to recapture the slaves, but they did not succeed. The determined slaves were able to sur-

Many descendants of African slaves live in the interior and follow unique ethnic customs.

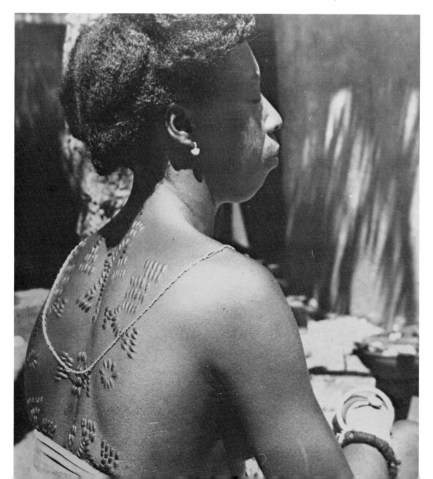

vive and to hide in the swamps and dense forest (known as the bush). Eventually, they formed villages and established groups similar to their African tribes. Descendants of these escaped slaves live in the interior today.

One of the slave leaders, Kwaku, is remembered for his contributions to peace and honored by a statue in Paramaribo. After a successful plantation revolt in 1759, he and a fellow slave named Boston offered peace terms to the Dutch. They agreed to end their attacks on the plantations if the Dutch would give them a certain number of guns, axes, and saws every year. The Dutch did not take the offer seriously and offered the slaves combs, scissors, and knives instead. Insulted and angry, Boston wanted to attack the Dutch once again, but Kwaku argued that they should be patient and try to persuade the planters to consider the slaves' views seriously. This time the two were successful, and the colonists agreed to a one-year cease-fire. In 1760, the colonists and the slaves signed a peace treaty that allowed slaves to settle freely in the interior.

Years of slave revolts, combined with weak administration, slowed the colony's progress during the late 1700s. And in 1780, the Netherlands went back to war with England. For more than 30 years, France, England, and the Netherlands fought a series of wars, and for most of the period of 1796 to 1814 the British once again controlled Guiana. But at the end of the wars, in 1815, the Treaty of Vienna gave the territory back to the Netherlands. The colony was then named Dutch Guiana. Britain claimed the area to the west, which is now the independent country of Guyana. France took possession of the territory to the east, which it named French Guiana (it remains under the administration of France).

Dutch Guiana recovered only partially from the troubles of these difficult years. The plantation owners' incomes had suffered because they had lacked sufficient ships to export products during the wars. The plantations also suffered from lack of care because of the slave revolts.

In 1807, the British showed their disapproval of slavery by refusing to transport any more slaves to Dutch Guiana and other colonies. This left plantation owners with fewer workers each year. In response, the Dutch government gave extra help to its colony of Java in Indonesia, but not to Dutch Guiana. Terrible fires in the capital, epidemics of yellow fever and smallpox, and continued slave revolts further weakened the fragile colony. Yielding to the slaves' demands and to pressure from other countries, the Dutch abolished slavery in 1863.

For ten years after they were freed, all former slaves were required to work on their plantations for wages. Afterward, some elected to stay and earn more money, but most left to join their fellow Africans in the bush. The labor shortage forced many plantations to close. In 1832, there were 431 plantations in Dutch Guiana. By 1873, there were only 123.

To restore the economy, the Dutch brought in laborers from India, China, and Java. These immigrants signed contracts to work for five or more years on the plantations. During this time they earned wages, and not all of them returned home after their contracts expired.

The population of Dutch Guiana changed with the arrival of these new families. The white-dominated plantation economy based on slave labor gradually evolved into a multiracial, multiethnic farming and business society, although Dutch-owned companies still dominated the economy. Over the years, fewer plantations were farmed as the lumber and mining industries grew. However, Dutch Guiana continued to export sugar and other tropical products to Europe and the United States.

When World War I broke out in 1914, the United States became interested in developing Dutch Guiana's supply of bauxite because it needed aluminum. Mining in Dutch Guiana started in about 1917, and the first ore was shipped in 1922.

The Dutch colonial government managed all the affairs of Dutch Guiana. During the early 20th century, it established health and educational services that helped to raise the standard of living of Dutch Guiana's citizens. In 1866, residents who met strict voting requirements based on property ownership and education received the right to vote for a chamber of representatives, or parliament. Although the Dutch government still retained its authority over the colony, voting rights were the first step toward independence.

Independence and After

After World War II ended in 1945, many residents of Dutch Guiana began pressuring the Netherlands to grant independence to the colony. In 1949, the Dutch government lifted voting restrictions in the colony, enabling all citizens to vote for parliament and to form political parties. In 1954, the Netherlands transferred complete control over Dutch Guiana's internal affairs to the parliament, an elected prime minister, and his Council of Ministers (an appointed cabinet), retaining control only of Dutch Guiana's foreign and defense policies.

Not everyone in Dutch Guiana agreed on the issue of independence from the Netherlands. Some political leaders argued that the country would be better off remaining a colony, because the Dutch administration was generous with financial assistance and the people had a high standard of living. Strongly opposed to continued Dutch rule was the political party dominated by the Creoles—descendants of African slaves who formed Dutch Guiana's largest and most influential ethnic group.

Creole leader Henck Arron (second from left) became the nation's first prime minister.

The road to self-rule was paved when the Creole leader Henck Arron, who had pledged to gain his land's independence, was elected prime minister in 1973. The Dutch government supported Arron and also promised about $100 million per year in development aid for ten years. On November 25, 1975, Dutch Guiana became the fully independent country of Suriname.

For the next five years, the government of Suriname operated under the constitution that political leaders had drafted just before independence. Under this constitution, the prime minister led the country, advised by his cabinet, as well as the popularly elected parliament, called the National Assembly. The constitution also called for an elected president, who served primarily as the ceremonial chief of state.

Money from the Netherlands supported work on a railroad, a hydroelectric station, and other operations related to the bauxite industry. The United States aided the newly independent country as well. It financed drainage and irrigation projects in the west that greatly extended Suriname's rice-growing capabilities.

Even so, the economy experienced trouble soon after independence. Between 1975 and 1980, about 150,000 people (almost one-third of the population), most of them well educated and affluent, decided to immigrate to the Netherlands. They feared that without Dutch administration, Suriname would fall into political and economic ruin. Because so many talented people left the country, many farms and businesses began to suffer. Teachers and workers in government and industry went on strike for higher salaries. At the same time, the worldwide demand for bauxite fell. This decreased the earnings Suriname could expect from its bauxite deposits and threatened its financial well-being. The American and Dutch companies involved in bauxite-mining operations were forced to pay higher taxes to operate their mines. As the economy slowed, unemployment rose.

On February 15, 1980, Suriname entered a period of rapid and sometimes violent political change. Just two days before regularly scheduled

In 1980, rebel soldiers staged a military coup, sending tanks into downtown Paramaribo.

general elections, the civilian government was overthrown in a military coup.

The problems that led to the coup had started almost a year before. A group of army sergeants had protested for some time about their low pay and lack of promotions. They wished to start a labor union, similar to ones in the Netherlands, to advance their cause. The prime minister had refused to allow this, and the sergeants had refused to work.

The leaders of the military coup were arrested and placed on trial. In response, 250 of their supporters in the army occupied a government building and a nearby park. On February 25, 1980, this group attacked the army's headquarters with automatic weapons and bazookas. It then sent armored tanks and trucks across the city to attack the civilian police headquarters. The rebels fired on the police from patrol boats on the Suriname River and burned the headquarters building to the ground. Several people were killed in these attacks. Because of the widespread destruction and chaos, the government lost its ability to maintain power. Many government officials left the country to avoid arrest.

After the attack, the small group of sergeants who had led the fighting found themselves in control. They had started with only one goal in mind—to receive higher pay and quicker promotions. Now they needed to organize people and programs quickly in order to carry on the business of government.

The new group called itself the National Military Council. It appointed a cabinet with civilian and military representatives and at first promised that government would soon be handed back to civilian authority. It formed a Policy Center made up of three military leaders and three civilians. But a few months later, the Policy Center dissolved the elected National Assembly and suspended the constitution. One of the original protestors, Desire D. Bouterse, took charge. He gained control of the army and soon became the most powerful figure in Suriname. He governed the country by decree—that is, by his own commands.

In December 1982, 15 citizens who had promoted a return to constitutional government were arrested and then executed without a trial. Both the Netherlands and the United States strongly protested by suspending their financial aid to Suriname. Though Suriname began to receive some aid from the Soviet Union and Cuba, the economy suffered.

By 1986, guerrilla groups began attacking economic targets in Suriname. The army responded by destroying villages and killing suspected insurgents. This civil war dragged on until 1991.

However, civilian rule did return to Suriname in 1987. Under heavy pressure because of the economic decline, the military relented. A new constitution was adopted by referendum, establishing a new legislative body called the National Assembly, to be elected by popular vote. In January 1988, a civilian president took office. The military ousted him in 1990, but elections were held again in 1991 and 1996. Though supporters of Bouterse were purged from the armed forces in 1995 and 1996, Bouterse's political party still has considerable influence over the government.

Suriname's diverse society includes people from Africa, Asia, Europe, and the Middle East. Many Javanese people live in the coastal fishing villages.

People

The people of Suriname represent a varied mixture of ethnic and racial backgrounds. The population of about 436,000 consists of seven distinct groups. Except for a small Indian population, all Surinamese are descended from immigrants. Citizens of Suriname include descendants of African slaves; Hindus, Javanese, and Chinese (most descended from contract laborers brought in by the Dutch); Europeans; and a small number of Middle Easterners from Lebanon and Syria.

Traditionally, these groups have clustered in separate cultural, religious, and political organizations. Although most have kept the religions and some of the customs of their original homelands, the various groups have lived together in remarkable harmony over the years. There is little prejudice, and marriage between men and women of different groups is common.

Whatever their ethnic background, the people of Suriname form close-knit families that care for each other and for older relatives. Very few women work outside their homes except as teachers, nurses, or shopkeepers. Women have not usually been active in Suriname's politics, although in 1982 a group of 1,000 women marched in the streets of the capital to protest the government's execution of a group of politically active civilians. By law, women have equal access to education, employment, and property. But customs and social pressures have limited their full exercise of these rights, especially regarding marriage and inheritance.

The Bouterse government tried to build on the harmony among peoples of different races and religions by promoting the concept of *amoksie*, or "mixture." It renamed the central square of the capital Unity Square. Suriname also has a holiday called National Unity Day, on July 1. The major national holiday, however, is Independence Day, November 25.

Language

Suriname's many languages reflect its ethnic diversity. Everyone knows at least some Dutch because it is the official language of the schools, the government, and the newspaper. English is spoken by many and understood by even more. Hindus speak Hindi as their ancestors did in India, those whose ancestors came from the island of Java speak Javanese, and the Chinese also speak their own language. To solve communication problems, the people of Suriname long ago developed a popular language that is understood and spoken by all. It is called Sranan Tongo, or Suriname Tongue Language, but is most commonly referred to either as Sranan or, colloquially, as Taki-Taki.

An English captain named John Stedman, who lived in central Guiana from 1773 to 1778, described Sranan as "so sweet, so sonorous and soft that the genteelest Europeans [here] speak little else." His description of the language encouraged others to write articles, stories, and poetry in Sranan. In 1960, the government added a Sranan verse to the national anthem.

Sranan is a mixture of English, Portuguese, Dutch, and Spanish sounds and words. It is not difficult to learn because its grammar is simple and its vocabulary is small. And because it is primarily a spoken language, spelling is not standardized—the same words can be written in different ways.

Because Suriname has developed independently, far away from Europe, Suriname Dutch is somewhat different from the language spoken in the Netherlands. Dutch and Sranan influence each other, and both are changing. Sranan used to be based primarily on the English language but now contains more Dutch words. Perhaps it will eventually become a new national language.

Religion

Each immigrant group that came to Suriname brought along its own religion. Today, no one religious group is dominant, and all faiths are respected. Hindus, Roman Catholics, Protestants from a variety of denominations, Muslims (followers of the Islamic religion), and Jews all practice their faiths freely in Suriname.

The religions of the Surinamese are evident in Paramaribo, where churches, mosques, temples, and synagogues abound.

One way to glimpse the variety of people in Suriname is to visit the churches, temples, and mosques in and around the capital city of Paramaribo. The Surinamese claim that the Roman Catholic cathedral is the largest church made entirely of wood in South America. The inside walls are of unpainted cedar, and the high ceilings are supported by wooden pillars. Light streams in from tall glass windows, each with a different pattern.

Lutherans and members of the Moravian Brethren join other Protestant religious communities in the capital. The largest Protestant congregation meets in the Dutch Reformed Church, an eight-sided building where pews are placed right on top of old gravestones. Queen Juliana of the Netherlands attended services here the day Suriname gained independence.

The ruins of one of the oldest synagogues in the Western Hemisphere are about two hours away from Paramaribo. It was built in 1665 by the Portuguese Jews who found refuge here from persecution in Brazil. Modern synagogues now flourish in the capital.

Followers of Hinduism form the largest religious group in Suriname. No area is very far from a Hindu temple filled with images of gods and goddesses in many forms, including cows, elephants, and dancing figures with many arms.

Muslims pray at the many mosques that also dot Suriname's horizon. In other countries, a religious leader calls Muslims to prayer from the top of the minaret, or tower, of the mosque. In Suriname, however, where the majority of Muslims are Javanese, they follow the custom of their homeland and await the sound of a drum from the mosque steps to call them to their weekly Friday service.

Creoles

The term Creole is used in Suriname to describe all descendants of African slaves who live on the coastal plain—one of the largest and most influential of Suriname's population groups. Most Creoles practice Chris-

Many of Suriname's Creoles grew up on plantations, where they learned farming skills.

tianity. A large majority have intermarried with members of other racial and ethnic groups. Thus, the 31 percent of the population defined as Creoles includes people of very different backgrounds.

In the 19th century, Creoles ran most of the large sugar, coffee, and cacao plantations. Many grew up on the plantations, where they learned the skills needed to farm efficiently.

The customs of the Creoles derive from their African heritage and their lives on the plantations. They live in large family groups, and everyone takes part in raising the children. Women tend to make the important family decisions. Many mothers spend little money on themselves so that they can afford to give their children higher educations.

Creole cooking uses roots and root vegetables similar to those grown in West Africa. One popular dish, called *pom*, is a combination of chicken, tomatoes, lemon juice, and ground *tajers*—a local root vegetable. Another specialty is rice, banana, breadfruit, codfish, and cassava (a fleshy vegetable root) all cooked together. It is called *er'eri*, which means "whole." Creoles also make a delicious peanut soup.

Creole festivities are extensions of family life. Birthdays are extremely important. Elaborate parties are given, especially for older people when they reach ages ending in zero. These *bigi jari* (big year) parties include not only family but a wide circle of friends as well. At a bigi jari celebration, the person being honored is the one who brings the cake.

At such a party, the older women may wear the *kotomisi*, the traditional Creole costume. This involves many layers of undergarments beneath a long, colorful dress with a wide skirt. The most distinctive feature of the costume is a large piece of heavily starched cotton cloth tied and knotted on the head. These large and colorful headpieces speak a language of their own. They can be tied and folded to send messages, such as "Meet me at the corner," to those who know how to interpret them.

Creoles live throughout the coastal plain and are involved in all walks of life, including farming, business, government, teaching, medicine, and law. Hard work and a determination to educate their children have greatly improved the lives of countless Creoles over the last 100 years.

Hindus

Hindus, who originally came from India as contract laborers for plantation owners, make up 37 percent of the population. They continue to speak Hindi and have retained many of the traditions of northern India, where most of their ancestors were born. These traditions revolve largely around the practice of their religion, Hinduism.

Hindus participate in frequent religious festivals. Every temple has at least one ceremony a year to honor the particular god to whom it is dedicated. The most important festivals, however, are celebrated in the streets of villages and cities, and everyone is welcome to join in.

There are four Hindu New Year celebrations—one for each season of the year. The most important one is Deepavali, a four-day Festival of Lights held in the fall. After they have thoroughly cleaned their homes, Hindus set out tiny clay lamps to welcome the goddess of prosperity. Candles flicker all over the towns and cities to celebrate the new year. Children and adults set off firecrackers to frighten away evil spirits, businessmen start new account books, and everyone eats candy and cakes to celebrate.

Holi Phagwa, the spring Fire Festival, is held on March 1. During this carnival-like festival, people delight in throwing colored powders and water on each other and all who walk by. Many arrive home with clothes and hair stained a brilliant red. At night, everyone goes to huge bonfires where stuffed likenesses of evil demons burn against the sky.

Drawing on their Indian background, Hindus flavor the rice, chicken, and vegetables that grow in Suriname with homemade spice mixtures such as curry and garam masala. One popular dish is *roti*, a baked breadlike pancake stuffed with curried chicken and potatoes. The roti can be cooked out-of-doors in a *tandoor*, a hollow clay oven with an open top. A wood fire below the tandoor heats the sides to such a high temperature that a flat piece of bread dough thrown on the inside wall cooks in 30 seconds.

Some Hindus cultivate small rice farms in the western coastal area, but large numbers have moved to the towns and cities. They believe strongly that families should work and save money together to make better lives for themselves. In particular, they usually insist that their children receive a good education so that they can enter any profession they choose.

Javanese

About 15 percent of the Surinamese are Javanese whose ancestors came from the island of Java. Like Suriname, Java was once a Dutch colony but now is part of Indonesia. Like the Hindus and Chinese, the Javanese were hired as contract laborers in the late 1800s. The Dutch on Java exported the workers as part of their regular trade with the plantation owners in Dutch Guiana. Today, Suriname has the only large Javanese settlement in the Americas.

A large number of Javanese families are still involved in farming. Some live in the capital, but most work in rice polders in the west or in

This young woman's ancestors came to Suriname from Java, an island in Indonesia.

farming and fishing villages all along the coast. Others live and work on the last large sugar plantation in Suriname.

Children speak Javanese at home and are taught to help perform family chores. For some children, this means leaving school when they reach age 12. Others receive more education and pursue a variety of occupations.

Javanese life centers around the home, which a Muslim religious leader blesses before the family moves in. The simplest Javanese home is the pina hut, made of pina palm branches. Palm-leaf roofs and a mud floor complete the structure. A second type of home is made of wood and has either a thatched palm-leaf or a ridged-iron roof. Rain pipes on the roof lead to water barrels that store water for dry-season drinking and cooking. The third, most modern style of home is constructed of wood and has glass windows. All of these houses are on wooden stilts or concrete pillars 3 to 9 feet (.9 to 2.7 meters) high to avoid flooding in the rainy season.

Javanese farming families usually keep a few cows and goats to supply themselves with meat and dairy products. They also have ducks, geese, or chickens, and they trade eggs for other foods in short supply.

An elaborate Indonesian dish called *rijsttafel*, or "rice table," is the center of festive occasions. The meal consists of bowls of boiled and fried rice accompanied by 15 or more side dishes of spiced meats and vegetables, such as stews made of pork and beef, toasted coconut, hot red-pepper sauces, and pickled cucumbers. An especially popular Javanese dish is *satay*, which is usually made with pieces of grilled pork in a spicy ground-peanut sauce.

Javanese Muslims follow the teachings of their religion's holy book, the Koran, but many of them also believe that spirits who live in plants, flowers, rivers, and trees dominate the world and that other powerful spir-

Devout Muslims, the Javanese built many mosques in Suriname. Many Javanese also follow traditional beliefs not found in the Koran (the Muslim holy book).

its live in places such as houses, knives, and musical instruments. The Javanese hold religious ceremonies in their homes and try to keep a peaceful relationship between themselves and the spirit world.

The marriage ceremony of a Javanese couple is a week-long event combining beliefs in the Koran and the spirits. Traditionally, parents arrange the wedding only on a day that is favorable to the spirits. Family members and friends spend three days at the bride's house before the ceremony on the fourth day. On one of these days, guests are invited to a ritual at the groom's house, during which water is poured over his head. They then move to the bride's home to anoint her with water.

Before friends dress the bride on her wedding day, they offer rice and bananas to the spirits. The women then grease her hair with coconut oil. They also paint the top of her forehead black and decorate it with gold, red, and blue sequins. Gold coins, bracelets, earrings, a golden comb, and flowers in her hair add to the bride's beauty.

In a traditional wedding, the bride waits in her own home while the men go to the religious ceremony, where the groom promises to support and care for his new wife. In modern weddings, both attend the ceremony. When the groom arrives at the bride's house, they share rice from the same bowl. The guests spend the three days that follow the wedding watching puppet shows, stage plays, or traditional Javanese dancing.

During the Muslim holy month of Ramadan, called Pasa in Suriname, observers do not eat between sunrise and sunset. When Pasa ends, a holiday begins. Celebrators wear some new piece of clothing if they can, and women put on their finest jewelry. Because the Muslim religious calendar depends on the phases of the moon instead of on the 12-month Julian calendar, this festival falls on a different date every year.

Chinese and Europeans

Large numbers of Chinese went to Suriname as plantation workers, but most returned home when their contracts ended. For this reason, Chinese now make up only about 2 percent of Suriname's population.

Some Chinese own small industrial and mining businesses in the hills near the capital city. Within the city, others run many shops and restaurants. Chinese food is popular, especially *moksie metie*, a locally invented dish of cooked meat served over rice.

An equally small number of Europeans also live and work in Suriname. A few Portuguese (from Portugal and Brazil), Dutch, Lebanese, Jews, and others form a small European-Middle Eastern minority.

People of the Rain Forest

Two different ethnic groups inhabit Suriname's dense rain forest zone south of the coastal plain. They are the Indians and the Maroon societies. Small bands of Indians roam the interior forest to which their ancestors retreated when European colonists forced them from the coast. Maroon societies—whose name comes from the term "maroon," used for black slaves who chose freedom in the bush over life on the plantations—live along the river banks.

About 8,000 native Arawaks, Caribs, Oayanas, and Trios dwell in the interior forest, living very much the way their ancestors did. Each tribe speaks its own language, yet the groups have many traditions in common. They grow food according to an ancient practice called slash-and-burn agriculture: they first slash, or clear, brush from land in the rain forest and then burn the brush to fertilize the soil. When the soil is no longer fertile, they move their homes to another site near running water and clear new

The Indians of the interior build simple shelters from wood, branches, and grasses.

SCENES OF
SURINAME

➤ *Workers plant rice, Suriname's staple food and a major export, in irrigated fields.*

Ⅴ *Brokopondo Lake, a small lake in northeastern Suriname, is encircled by forest.*

◄ *Almost half of the population lives in the port city of Paramaribo, the capital.*

∨ *Surrounded by lush gardens, this lavish home in Paramaribo serves as the residence of Suriname's prime minister.*

➤ *A plume of red and black feathers crowns the forest-dwelling royal fly catcher.*

◄ *The banks of the Coppename River are lush with reeds, trees, and other vegetation.*

⅄ *In the forested interior, rivers serve as roadways for the people of the Maroon societies.*

➤ *The Surinamese are very religious, and churches are found in the remotest areas.*

➤ People of all ethnic groups bargain for food at the Central Market in Paramaribo.

➤ Suriname's native American Indians produce distinctive earthenware jugs and pots.

➤ Guides help visitors explore Suriname's more than 60,000 square miles (156,000 square kilometers) of undeveloped land.

◄ *With their Dutch architecture, many homes in Paramaribo recall a colonial past.*

◄ *Suriname's bauxite mines and refining plants provide much of the world's aluminum.*

➤ *The forests that cover 90 percent of the land have created a lumber industry.*

(continued from page 48)

flutes to accompany the ceremony, in which the young men wear padded cotton jackets filled with live ants or wasps while they perform a long dance to purge their bodies of evil substances.

Some Indians live near populated areas and sell their goods to city-dwellers. Even those deep in the forest trade handicrafts, fish, and lumber with outsiders. Villagers grow cotton and plants that produce a red dye, and use the two to make colored textiles to wear or sell. The women weave ropes and baskets from grasses.

Maroon Societies

Descendants of the African slaves who escaped to the forest and fought the Dutch for their freedom make up about 10 percent of the total population of Suriname. The communities created by the escaped slaves are called Maroon societies. Such groups also exist in other areas of South America, but the six tribes of Suriname form the largest Maroon population in existence.

During their 200 years in the wild bushland of the interior, these independent people have preserved and developed their African culture and languages. A *granman* (chief) rules over each settlement. He interviews and then welcomes or rejects any white person who wishes to visit his village. The chiefs, who are both political and religious leaders, are responsible for relations with the government of Suriname.

Most of the villages are located on the rivers south and southeast of the capital. In each, 100 to 200 people live in huts. The men marry from one to three wives, but divorce is frequent. Both men and women are allowed to marry again. Children usually stay with their mother until the age of six, at which time most boys go to live with an uncle on the mother's side. This uncle teaches them hunting, fishing, and other survival skills.

Men hunt wild game and fish with bows and arrows tipped with poison. With an arrow attached to a string, they pull deadly piranha from the water and leave them to die. The fish taste delicious cooked over a hot fire.

space for crops. Because the groups keep moving, they build simple huts of forest materials, some open on the sides. Sleeping hammocks are hung across the hut. Some huts have a stool for sitting, but most people prefer to sit on the cleared floor or in a hammock. Also within the hut are a few homemade earthenware pots, decorated with simple geometric shapes, which are used for storage and cooking.

Women are responsible for cooking the food. One time-consuming chore is the daily preparation of cakes made from cassava. Only the sweet variety of cassava root can be eaten straight from the ground. The most common kind of cassava contains a poison that must be removed before cooking, and its preparation is an ancient ritual. Women first peel and grate the roots, then cover the mixture with a heavy object. They hang the cassava in a bag over a bowl into which the poisonous juice slowly drips. When the juice is all gone, the remaining cassava meal is toasted and made into a flat bread.

Indian men train dogs to help them hunt game animals in the forest. They also use spears and arrows dipped in a powerful poison that they extract from plants in an ancient, carefully guarded secret process. Monkeys high up in the trees topple to the ground when pierced with one of these arrows. The Indians skin the monkeys and then cook them over an open fire.

Fishing, like hunting, is carried out in traditional ways. One simple technique is to trap fish in large baskets. Another method is used to capture a whole school of fish for village consumption: the fishermen release into the water a poison that causes the fish to stop breathing. Boys and girls wade in to collect the fish that float to the surface. The poison is harmless to humans, so the fish can be eaten fresh that day or dried for later use. Young boys also climb tall forest trees to capture honey—a prized delicacy.

When the boys grow older, they achieve manhood by enduring an initiation rite overseen by the tribal chief and the medicine man, who serves as a religious leader. Villagers gather in a circle, playing drums and

(continued on page 57)

The houses of the Maroon people are small structures made of wood and palm fronds.

In the Maroon societies, a woman usually owns a house in the village where she grew up, another house built by her husband, and a third in a camp in the forest where she stays when she is planting. Women lead independent lives and are responsible for raising food in cleared areas some distance from the village. They travel to these plots in their own canoes. Like the Indians, the Maroons clear a new plot when the old one is no longer fertile.

The Maroon people at first established their food camps far from the villages in order to prevent white people from discovering them and recapturing the escaped slaves. Even though the need no longer exists, the tradition of separating the camp from the village still continues.

Women grow sweet potatoes, plantains, bananas, okra, corn, sugarcane, and tobacco. Another specialty is a kind of rice that grows on dry land, rather than in flooded fields. A typical meal consists of rice or cake, a piece of meat or fish, and a vegetable sauce. In the village, women cook the meal and bring it to a house where the men eat together. Women eat more informally in their own houses with the children.

Many village houses are just big enough for a sleeping hammock to be strung from one side to the other. Others have two small rooms. The walls are of woven palm fronds or cut wooden planks. The roofs are palm-frond matting. The floors are made of mud, and exterior trenches dug around the house prevent flooding. Because the houses are so small, all cooking is done outdoors. Villagers clear the underbrush around their huts and plant orange, lime, mango, banana, and coconut trees. Some keep chickens.

The Maroon tribal societies in Suriname are sometimes called "river people," because they depend on the rivers for survival. The skill that has most aided their survival has been boat building. All men and women own dugout canoes, which transport them safely and efficiently through Suriname's rivers—the only "roads" in the forest.

Dugout canoes range from 25 to 45 feet (8 to 14 meters) in length and are carved from a single tree. The boat builder first strips the bark of a tree and leaves the trunk to dry. He then hollows out the dried log in the shape of a canoe with an adz, a long-handled tool that resembles a small hoe. The log canoe is then ready to be burned and stretched. The builder starts a fire inside the hollow tree. He keeps the fire at the right temperature by adding dry leaves or water. He cools the outside of the shell with a cover of mud and wet leaves.

Maroon men carve boats, tools, and ceremonial instruments from the forest hardwoods.

Dugout canoes are made as they have been for centuries.

When the wood is warm and pliable, the builder can easily stretch and shape it. To hold the shape, men work together to put stays across the width of the canoe, being careful not to crack the outside shell. They then drive wooden stakes into the ground and dry the boat inside the stakes. The owner removes the dry boat from the mold and then decorates each end with carvings, paintings, or pieces of brightly colored metal.

These dugout canoes are so well balanced that while one person paddles, another can move about to probe the riverbed with a long, straight stick. Very large dugouts can be equipped with outboard motors to haul heavy supplies, such as timber. Men provide a major source of village income by working for sawmills in the forest, felling, stripping, and transporting trees. After they load their canoes at the mill, the men travel four to five days to the coast to market the wood.

The Maroon societies, like the Indians, accept medical care and education from Christian missionaries, but most still follow their ancestral

African religions. The river people of Suriname wear an *obeah*, or charm, in the form of a bracelet or necklace of shells, fiber, or grass, to protect themselves from danger.

Small houses in every village serve as shrines where medicine men offer prayers to ancestors. Ceremonies mark births, marriages, and deaths, and villagers stop at their shrines daily to communicate with their gods. Men and women covered in sacred white-clay powder sing and chant to cure others of physical problems or to fight evil spirits. Every village is guarded by palm fronds to keep away evil spirits, and an obeah man (one who practices a form of voodoo) dances and chants to purify any stranger who enters.

The friendship that exists today between the river people and the Indians began in the 18th century, when the Indians helped slaves who had escaped to the jungle to hide. They also shared their knowledge of plant medicines and poisons with the Africans. In return, the Africans showed the natives how to use the metal tools they had brought with them and how to make sturdier wooden canoes. As their numbers grew, the Africans sometimes raided Dutch villages for tools and traded them for Indian hammocks, baskets, and bows and arrows.

Today, these two groups continue to support and befriend each other, but they still maintain separate lives. The Indian way of life lies deep in the forest, while the Maroon people live and voyage on the rivers.

Though the Dutch influence lingers in the architecture of this government building in Paramaribo, Suriname is proudly independent.

Government and Education

From 1815 to 1975, the Dutch held colonial Suriname, then called Dutch Guiana. For the last 21 years of that period, residents controlled its internal affairs. However, many groups campaigned for complete independence. The movement succeeded in 1975, when the Netherlands relinquished its hold over Dutch Guiana, which then became the fully self-governing country of Suriname. The first Surinamese government—led by elected, nonmilitary officials—continued to operate under the parliamentary system. Political unrest tested the civilian regime several times over the years. In 1980, Surinamese military forces successfully overthrew the civilian regime and took charge of the country. Lieutenant Colonel Bouterse emerged as the leader of this military government and also became the commander of Suriname's army.

A few months later, Commander Bouterse's regime suspended the country's constitution and terminated the citizens' right to vote. It also dissolved the National Assembly. In 1984, Bouterse created a new assembly called the Supreme Council, but its 33 members were not elected by popular vote. Instead, Bouterse appointed them from military, labor, and business organizations. Under this system, Bouterse maintained absolute power in Suriname, using the strength and weapons of the army to enforce his policies.

In the summer of 1986, however, Bouterse appointed a new Council of Ministers to work with the Supreme Council to prepare a new constitution. For the first time since 1980, members of the three largest political parties in Suriname were included in the process. These parties represented the country's Creole, Hindu, and Javanese populations.

The new constitution was submitted to popular referendum and approved by 93 percent of the voters in 1987. Elections for a new National Assembly were held later that year, and a civilian president took office in 1988. Though the military interfered again in 1990, removing the president and his government from office, new elections were held again in 1991 and 1996.

Under the 1987 constitution, the 51 members of the National Assembly are popularly elected for 5-year terms. A two-thirds majority of the Assembly then selects the president, who also serves for a 5-year term. If two-thirds of the members cannot agree on a candidate, a larger People's Assembly is formed, including all the National Assembly delegates as well as elected regional and municipal representatives; this larger body needs only a simple majority to select a president.

The president appoints a 16-member cabinet to carry out the oper-

Medical care is hard to get for people who live in the forested areas of the interior.

ations of government. There is also a 14-member State Advisory Council to advise the president about the conduct of policy. Most of the seats on this council are distributed by a system of proportional representation among the political parties represented in the National Assembly.

The Ministry of Public Health is responsible for health and welfare; however, private and religious groups support most of Suriname's medical programs. Religious communities operate several hospitals and deliver medical help to seriously ill inhabitants in remote areas.

During the colonial period, the Dutch established excellent hospitals, seven of which are now run by the government. Equipment is limited, especially in the rural parts of the country, and medications are sometimes unavailable. But hospitals are clean and run efficiently by nurses and doctors. Overall, there is one doctor for every 1,350 people.

The government requires children between the ages of 6 and 12 to go to school. City children wear uniforms and attend school regularly. Children in the Indian villages near the coast dress very informally. Their schools have iron roofs to keep off the rain but are open to breezes on all sides. Inside, the students sit on a brushed earth floor in front of a blackboard. In the remote villages of the interior, children usually do not attend school at all, despite the law.

Education for all children has helped the ethnic groups of Suriname to understand each other by encouraging a standard language. Many young people speak only Hindi or Javanese at home. Although most also know Sranan, that language is more often spoken than written. In school, teachers and pupils use Dutch. All textbooks and other reading materials are in Dutch, so all students learn and share the same language. English is also taught in schools and is widely understood.

Religious groups operate many schools in Suriname and are given some financial support by the government. There are about 225 primary schools and 90 secondary schools in the country. The University of Suriname was established in 1966. It offers training for teachers and courses in law, medicine, the social sciences, agriculture, forestry, mining, and other disciplines.

During the military-based regime of Desire Bouterse (third from left), the Suriname government was often accused of violating human rights.

Skilled teachers are difficult to find in Suriname today because many left for the Netherlands after independence. Thus, many of the young people who study in the primary and secondary schools of Suriname are ill prepared to enter the university and must take extra training in evening classes in order to do so. In 1982, about 80 percent of the people could read and write. The percentage declined in the 1980s, but rebounded to about 93 percent by 1995.

In addition to health and education, human rights are a major concern as Suriname works toward a stable and progressive democracy. During the reign of Bouterse's military government in the 1980s, several foreign countries expressed concern about denial of human rights in Suriname, and the abuses were detailed in the report of a commission appointed by the Organization of American States (OAS). The government often disregarded citizens' right to trial, denied them the freedom to attend public meetings, and censored the media. Opponents of the government were accused of political crimes. Since Suriname's return to constitutional rule in the early 1990s, the civilian government has taken steps to limit the political power of the military and to reestablish respect for basic human rights.

After independence in 1975, eight daily newspapers continued to serve Suriname's multilingual society. Newspapers were printed in Dutch, Hindi, Javanese, Chinese, and English. Several Dutch journalists were always in the capital reporting on people and events in Suriname. Radio stations and six television stations were located in cities and towns across the coastal plain. People had their choice of AM and FM stations broadcasting in all the languages of Suriname, including Sranan.

After the military takeover, the government announced that all newspapers and radio and television broadcasts would be censored, and it took control of the media. Some media offices were simply destroyed. Soon Suriname had only one newspaper, two radio stations, and one television station, all run by government-appointed officials.

Since the resumption of civilian rule, the rebuilding process has been slow, hampered by the country's economic problems. By the mid-1990s, however, Suriname had two privately owned newspapers and about 20 radio stations, mostly under private control. Continued growth of independent media outlets should contribute greatly to the free expression of ideas in Suriname.

The economy depends heavily on revenues from the mining and refining of bauxite.

Economy

The low hills in the forests of Suriname contain one of the world's richest supplies of bauxite. These extensive reserves are important to Suriname because bauxite is the source of aluminum—one of the most-used metals in the world. Bauxite is mined in the coastal plain at Moengo and in the hills southeast of Paramaribo at Paranam. About 85 percent of Suriname's export income comes from the mining and refining of bauxite.

Bauxite was first discovered at Moengo in the early 1900s. The ore there lies so near the surface that, in the first few years, mining was done with a pick and shovel. Moengo is still one of the most productive bauxite-mining areas in Suriname.

It takes about 2 tons (2.2 metric tons) of bauxite to make 1 ton (1.1 MT) of alumina. The alumina is then chemically changed by electricity to make about .5 ton (.55 MT) of aluminum. This final phase requires large amounts of electric power. Because water power is the cheapest source of electrical energy, aluminum producers try to locate plants near a plentiful source. The Suriname Aluminum Company, or SURALCO (a subsidiary of ALCOA, the Aluminum Company of America) constructed a massive hydroelectric power station on the Suriname River at Afobaka. SURALCO and Billiton, a Dutch company, use power generated by this dam to convert alumina into aluminum.

The Afobaka Dam took six years to construct and was completed in 1965. Its power station is located in a concrete center section. The rest of the dam is made of clay, sand, and rock. Most of the energy generated by the power station is used to produce aluminum. A smaller amount is used by the government to supply power to the surrounding area.

Bauxite is still Suriname's most important source of foreign revenue. But bauxite mining and refining have decreased since 1975, when production was cut because a fall in world demand lowered the price of aluminum in international markets. Suriname's economy has shown little growth since 1978, largely because of the decline in bauxite production.

Other minerals found in Suriname, such as iron ore, manganese, copper, nickel, and platinum, are not plentiful enough to be mined commercially. Gold lies in the mountains, but in quantities too small to support commercial mining operations. Individual prospectors still find gold in Suriname, and it is possible that some gold remains undiscovered.

Farming employs about 15 percent of Suriname's work force. Sugarcane and citrus fruits, particularly oranges, grow well in the coastal plain. Although these were once export crops, the international market for them has become so limited that most of the produce is now consumed within

Alumina is converted into aluminum at this SURALCO plant; it is then exported.

the country. Most sugarcane is grown on a state-owned plantation in Marienburg.

Rice grows in the drained marshes, particularly in the western district of Coronie. Because rice needs constant flooding to develop properly, water is sent through the ditches during the dry seasons to irrigate the marshes and to dilute any saltwater that has crept in from the sea. About three-quarters of all agricultural land is devoted to growing rice, which is the staple food of Suriname. Large amounts of the crop are consumed at home. Yet the polders are so fertile and well suited to rice that sometimes as much as 50 percent of the crop can be exported. Because Suriname's climate is so warm, rice is planted and harvested all during the year.

In the early 1950s, Dutch officials established an experimental rice farm in Wageningen, in the northwestern rice-growing region. The mechanized plantation they created today yields the world's largest crops, producing about one-third of all the rice in Suriname. The plantation is government-owned, but its facilities also process rice for private owners.

Ridges of sandy soil running parallel to the coast are planted with coffee, cacao, soybeans, and peanuts. Coffee and cocoa (the product of the cacao tree), once exported, are now grown only for domestic use. Peanuts and soybeans are good sources of protein for the Surinamese, who depend heavily on vegetables. Corn, sweet potatoes, tomatoes, cabbage, and cassava are all raised for domestic use. Machines to cultivate the soil and methods to control disease have improved crop production.

Bananas and coconuts are grown for export. Coconuts are used as food for humans and animals and can also be pressed into vegetable oil. Palm oil, made from coconuts and from the nuts of other palm trees, has been processed and exported by the Surinamese since the 1970s. The government is supporting increased production of palm oil, which is used to make soaps and candles. A white oil from the inner portion of the nut is also used to produce margarine.

To preserve their croplands, farmers must constantly clear the forest that borders the narrow coastal strip. Although they have always kept

Suriname has only begun to tap its greatest resource—trees that can be cut for lumber.

chickens and other domestic fowl and have raised sheep, goats, and pigs for food and to sell at market, the farmers have traditionally been interested in clearing coastal land to grow rice rather than to create grazing lands for cattle. Many have simply grazed their herds on the poor grass of the swamps, where the low level of nutrients results in inferior cattle. During the years of its administration, the Dutch government set up experimental cattle-breeding farms to provide better supplies of meat and milk to the population.

Fish caught in the rivers and drainage ditches of the rural areas are nutritious additions to the diet of the Surinamese. A fishing industry has developed, based on the abundance of shrimp in the coastal waters. More shrimp than fish are now caught in Suriname. The shrimp exported from modern packing plants are an important part of the economy.

Trees are one of Suriname's greatest natural resources. Forests cover more than 90 percent of the country, but development of the timber industry has been limited by a lack of investment. The government now owns the sawmills that Dutch companies had operated in Suriname since the colonial period. It pays workers and managers and uses profits from the business as income for the state. Plywood and other wood products are important exports, earning some of the foreign exchange the country needs to buy other goods.

More than 2,000 varieties of trees grow in the rain forests of Suriname, but only certain ones are suitable for building materials, furniture, and other wood products. Some of these, such as teak, cedar, and mahogany, are known throughout the world. Others, such as greenheart, mora, and letterwood, are little known outside the tropics. Wood from the mora tree is particularly sought after because it resists insects and moisture.

The Maroon people play an important part in the lumber industry. These forest-dwellers are expert at felling, stripping, and transporting trees. Skilled boatmen generally tie the logs to rafts constructed of light wood or to large dugout canoes and float them downriver, over rapids and around falls.

Despite its abundant natural resources, Suriname suffers from high foreign debt, high unemployment, lack of modern roads and houses, poor transportation facilities, and an inflation rate that has sometimes ballooned far out of control. In an attempt to deal with such problems, the military government in the 1980s expanded its authority over many aspects of the economy, regulating prices, exchange rates, imports, and

Fish are an important part of the diet and a growing industry along the coast.

exports. By 1994 about half of the work force was employed by the government or by state-owned companies. Yet the economy continued to suffer. Today, potential international investors would like to see the government liberalize its economic policies, control the deficit, and create a stable business environment. These conditions, however, are much easier to describe than to accomplish.

Transportation

Rivers served as the main arteries of transportation in Suriname in prehistoric and colonial times, and the country's rivers still far outnumber its roads. Because roads are expensive to build and difficult to maintain in this heavily forested country, the government has constructed highways only in the coastal zone. Only a few roads lead south to the interior, and most of these follow the natural contours of the river valleys.

In most areas of the country, the best possible method of travel is still the dugout canoe. The rock-filled rivers are so narrow in some places that boats larger than canoes cannot move quickly enough to avoid the obstacles that appear around every bend. When falls and rapids interrupt a river's flow, boatmen take the canoes out of the water and carry them around the dangerous spots. About 745 miles (1,200 kilometers) of rivers and canals are navigable by boats larger than canoes, but steamships and freighters cannot travel on most of Suriname's rivers.

Indians and European settlers were able to travel by boat along the coastal plain all the way from the Marowijne River on the eastern boundary to the Corantijn River in the west. The small streams and river branches on which they steered their boats were not wide, but most of them were quite deep. The settlers dug a few canals to make an inland waterway for transporting goods and slaves from one plantation to another. Crops and goods are still sent along this water road to Paramaribo today and are then shipped to Europe, South America, and the United States.

Huge tankers dock at Paramaribo to fill their holds with bauxite, rice, and other exports.

The settlers chose an excellent natural harbor on the Suriname River, about 14 miles (23 kilometers) upstream from the sea, as the site for Paramaribo. While the country was a Dutch colony, freighters and luxury liners used to dock there regularly with passengers for the Netherlands, the West Indies, and other ports.

Because the coastland is so flat, all of the coastal rivers spread out into mud banks as they flow into the sea. The Suriname River, which has the deepest channel, has been dredged even deeper in modern times so that freighters can carry bauxite all the way to the ocean. Tugboats assist these large vessels as they wind around the bends in the rivers. In the west, riverboats carry rice and bananas for export to the port of Nieuw Nickerie.

Only about 2,780 miles (4,470 kilometers) of main roads exist in Suriname. Some of these are paved, and some have a hard, gravel surface. But most are covered with sand, which is dusty in the dry season and muddy when it rains. There are four main roads; the most heavily traveled goes from Albina in the east to Nieuw Nickerie in the west. A second road runs across the coastal zone about 31 miles (50 km) farther south. A third leads southeast from Paramaribo to the bauxite-mining area, and the fourth runs along a hilly western section to the site of a high waterfall on the Corantijn River.

Some officials favor building a road south through the interior to the Brazilian border. Others feel that this would destroy the land and vegetation and would not bring the country any advantages in return. The environment certainly does not lend itself to road building: it would be difficult to supply workers with food and equipment, and the expense of cutting through the rain forest would be enormous. Upkeep of the roads in the forest area is an unending job, because the vegetation grows back almost as soon as it is cut. Thus, it seems unlikely that more roads will be built in the rain forest unless important natural resources are discovered that would make the expense worthwhile.

Paramaribo is the center of traffic in Suriname. Cars, buses, and trucks are driven on the left-hand side of the street—a remnant of the period when the British controlled Suriname. There are more motorized bicycles in the country than there are cars because the bicycles are cheaper and more efficient.

In the capital, workers and shoppers move around the city on buses. The buses tend to be hot and crowded, but they are also fast and less expensive than taxis. Taxicabs have no meters, so riders must arrange a

Paramaribo's clean, paved streets contrast with the overgrown paths of the interior.

fare with the driver in advance. Though it is possible to travel to other cities from the capital by bus, the trips are slow and often involve long waits.

There are two short railroad lines in Suriname, neither of which carries passengers. The total amount of track is 104 miles (167 kilometers). One western line runs from a small town on the Corantijn River into the Bakhuis Mountains. The other, which runs south of the capital into the interior, was built to transport men and equipment into the gold fields. But gold mining did not develop enough to make the line profitable, and part of the track leading into the capital has been removed.

There are several ways to enter Suriname. One is to take a ferry across the river from either Guyana or French Guiana. Usually, however, visitors arrive in Paramaribo by air. Zanderij International Airport, equipped for jet traffic, is one of the largest airports in South America. The United States government used it during World War II, when American troops were stationed in Suriname to protect the bauxite deposits at Moengo.

Because there are so few roads, air traffic within the country is particularly important. Small airports serve several cities and towns in the coastal plain, carrying mail and passengers. And the government has funded the construction of a limited number of airstrips in the interior, making some areas accessible for the first time.

Homes, shops, and government buildings crowd Paramaribo, where half of all Surinamese live.

Cities and Towns

About 90 percent of the people of Suriname live in a region that covers only 3 percent of the country's total area—the towns and villages along the coast. The capital and chief port of Suriname, Paramaribo, is the country's largest city and its center of activity. Approximately 201,000 people— almost one-half of the nation's population, a majority of them Creoles— live in and around the city. In the Sranan language, the city is called Foto (Fort), in honor of Fort Zeelandia, which has guarded the entrance to the Suriname River since 1650.

Most of the homes and office buildings standing in Paramaribo today were built after a terrible fire in 1821. A few imposing buildings are constructed of red brick. The rest are made of native wood painted white to reflect the sun. Old-style homes have porches on the second and sometimes even the third floor. These porches, supported by graceful wooden columns, are decorated with figures and designs of wood or wrought iron.

The city's main square is one of the most beautiful in South America. Its large, grassy center is surrounded by the Presidential Palace and other government buildings. Behind the palace is a magnificent garden with row after row of tall royal palms.

The tree-shaded streets of Paramaribo provide welcome relief from the hot and humid climate. Lined with mahogany trees or stately palms,

Many coastal villages look as they have for centuries, with simple wood-and-straw huts lining the shore.

they wind beside businesses, schools, hospitals, churches, and modern residences. Flowering trees add color to gardens, particularly the scarlet blooms of the flamboyant tree. The monkey-tree, sometimes called the raintree, has leaves that catch the dew at night. When the leaves open with the morning sun, the dew drops to the ground and waters the grass.

The Suriname Museum houses archaeological, cultural, and natural history exhibits. The military government closed the museum in the 1980s, and exhibits from all periods of the country's history were stored away in barrels. Since the return to civilian rule, the museum has once again been open to the public.

The lively central market in Paramaribo brings together all the people, foods, and customs of Suriname. Chinese, Hindus, Javanese, and Creoles buy and sell every kind of fish, meat, and vegetable available in the country. Food may be cooked to a customer's request right on the spot. Exotic spices are sold nearby.

Around the market are busy streets full of cars and people. Department stores stand next to souvenir and craft shops. Restaurants serve foods fresh from the market, cooked by chefs of many nationalities. At night, residents stroll along the Suriname River past foodstalls set up by Javanese merchants. Lighted by candles, the stalls offer inexpensive meat and vegetable dishes in a picturesque setting.

Not far from Paramaribo is the bauxite-mining town of Paranam. Old plantations dot the landscape along the river between the two towns. Farther south is the town of Afobaka, the site of the SURALCO hydroelectric dam and the huge, artificial Van Blommestein Lake. Nearby is the Brownsberg National Park.

East of Paramaribo, in the Commewijne District, the town of Nieuw Amsterdam is guarded by an old fortress. Javanese who live here in wooden homes set high on stilts work nearby at the last sugar plantation in Suriname. Farther east are Moengo, the bauxite-mining center, and Albina, a border town across the river from French Guiana. Tourists can take airplane and dugout-canoe trips from Albina to villages and nature reserves in the interior.

The road west of Paramaribo goes through forests of coconut palms to Totness, in the Coronie District. Farther west is the rice-growing area of Wageningen, and at the border of Guyana is Nieuw Nickerie, Suriname's second largest city and the home of a large Hindu population. This flat, humid area nurtures palm, banana, and rice plantations, orchids and flowering trees, and fierce mosquitoes.

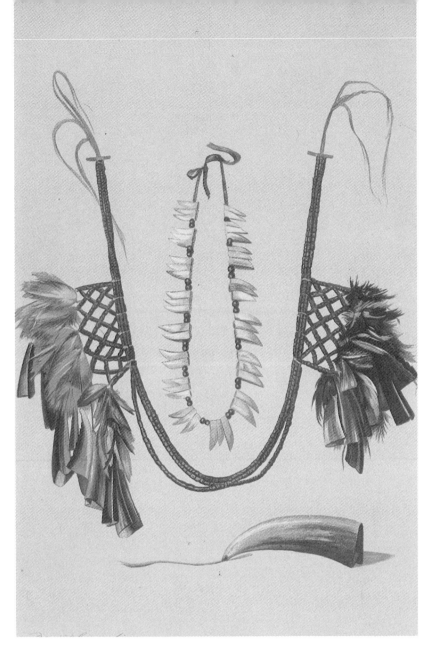

Each of Suriname's ethnic groups has its own artistic traditions. Indian artifacts include necklaces made from animal teeth and bird feathers.

Artistic Traditions

Much of the artistic life of Suriname is rooted in the cultural traditions of its major population groups: Creole, Hindus, Javanese, Maroon, and Indian. Artistic traditions in Suriname often have religious origins.

Javanese and Hindus have many similar cultural and religious traditions. Some Javanese in Suriname follow the Hindu religion. During Hindu festivals, stories taken from great Hindu legends are presented by male actors in public and private religious celebrations. The plays are meant to provide a good example for the audience. To convince people that the hero knows best, they always have a happy ending.

In a Javanese *wayang* (play), characters are portrayed by puppets made of leather or wood, or by human actors wearing masks. A storyteller narrates the dialogue and also manipulates the puppets. Sometimes the audience watches the play on a screen lighted from behind, so that it sees not the puppets but their shadows.

Javanese storytelling dances are famous all over the world. Dancers spend years training for their roles. They are not allowed to perform until they have mastered the correct and graceful ways to kneel, run, leap in the air, spin around, and make complicated movements with their hands, fingers, and eyes. Male and female dancers wear elaborate, colorful costumes and makeup. A dancer's headdress can be a spectacular and delicately balanced masterpiece, made with flowers, feathers, or even sticks of burning incense. Children attending a play festival sometimes join the festivities by wearing gold-colored crowns.

Javanese dances and plays are accompanied by an orchestra consisting mostly of percussion instruments. The *gamelan* and other instruments similar to xylophones and gongs provide the rhythm. Two-stringed instruments and flutes play the melody.

The Indians of the rain forest have their own form of music. Out of the materials of the forest they create drums and flutes to accompany their religious dances. They play their flutes either by holding them straight and blowing at one end or by holding them to the side and blowing with air from the nose. However they are played, the sound is haunting.

The large Creole population in the cities and towns is far removed from the traditional religious culture of its past. Still, ancient African music reinterpreted by Maroons and Creoles bursts forth daily in radio broadcasts and on festive occasions. The players beat skin-covered bongo drums to make music and, in the bush, to send messages through the air. During religious ceremonies in the interior, drums provide accompaniment as celebrants walk barefoot over coals from a fire.

Humans are not the only music makers. Birdsong competitions are a custom throughout Suriname. People can be seen on the streets carrying a songbird in a cage. The competitions are held on Sundays and holidays in public plazas and parks.

Aside from the religious festivals and private celebrations that include dance and drama, the cultural life of modern Suriname is relatively quiet. Occasional plays are presented in Dutch and Sranan at the Suriname Cultural Center in Paramaribo. Once or twice a year foreign groups, such as a Latin American band or Chinese acrobats, give performances. A few movie theaters show films in Chinese, Hindi, Javanese, Dutch, and English.

Occasionally, musicians give a public concert in the capital. More often, small musical groups meet at someone's home to play classical com-

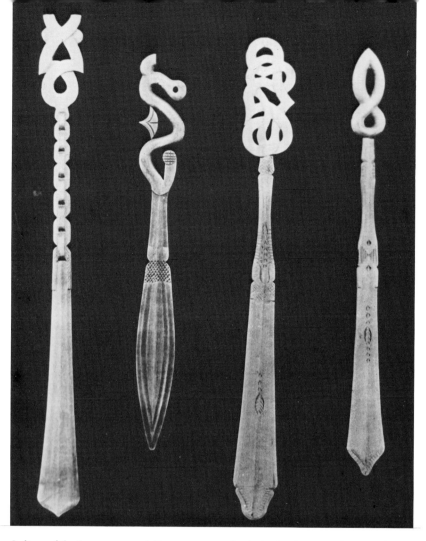

Indians of the Saramaccaner tribe are carvers who design intricate wooden utensils.

positions, jazz, or popular music. Indonesian and Hindu cultural centers offer instruction in native music, dance, and art.

Artistic creation is part of everyday life for many Surinamese. Before a Maroon woman bakes a large cassava cake, for example, she will draw a pattern on it. Those who share the cake later also will share the pleasure of this short-lived decoration and the message it contains.

The art of wood carving is highly developed among Maroon men, who make canoe paddles, drums, and furniture out of forest hardwoods. Some groups paint designs on their carvings.

When a wood carver makes an object, he works a message into his design. For departing friends, he may decorate a box with a circular carving of a vine surrounded by sharply pointed triangles. The circle made by the vine depicts a friendship that goes on forever. The triangles represent crocodile teeth, which signify that friendship must sometimes be defended. Large triangles around the edge represent kisses. A graceful branch flowing through the whole design is meant to encourage the friend never to forget the carver.

Maroon women exercise their creative talents by carving calabash (a type of gourd) shells into spoons, dishes, and bowls. First, the women scrape out the pulp from the fruit of the calabash tree. Then they boil and dry the shell. Once dry, the shell can be carved and decorated.

Many women are skilled at spinning thread and weaving it into cloth.

Craft shops in the capital stock a selection of products made by Surinamese of all ethnic groups. Indian baskets, which are particularly popular, range from shallow, wide baskets for shaking rice to deep, spacious containers. Creole tablecloths and napkins feature needlework designs that have specific meanings. A design may relate the history of some event, or it may send a message, such as "come back soon."

Javanese Surinamese make decorated batik cloth using the wax-resistant dye process their ancestors brought from their Indonesian homeland. In this time-consuming process, the artist makes designs on the cloth with a small, pencil-like piece of wax enclosed in a holder. The more skilled the artist, the more complicated and intricate the design. The artist then dips the cloth into dye (blue is a popular color) until the design appears in the non-waxed portions, and then washes the wax away. In a quicker, modern method, stamps made out of copper put the wax on the cloth. These patterns are not as interesting, but the process is faster and so the cost is lower.

The people of Suriname have long expressed themselves through painting and drawing. Art exhibits are common in the cities, and some artists have become well known in their own country and in the Netherlands.

Natives sometimes greet visitors to Suriname with letters of welcome decorated with dried leaves and flowers. This tradition may have been inspired by a woman who came to Suriname in 1684 with a Protestant religious group called the Labadists. Maria Sibylla Merian, a talented artist, collected samples of the caterpillars, butterflies, and insects of Suriname and of the flowers and plants on which they fed. Her book of beautifully detailed, colored drawings was published in 1705 and stands today as a treasured document of her adopted country.

Even as they struggle to modernize their nation, the Surinamese hold on to centuries-old traditions, such as the outdoor market.

Suriname– Past and Future

For many years, central Guiana remained isolated from countries overseas as well as from its neighbors in South America. Its thick forests and inhospitable waterways prevented inland travel. Only its coast provided access for European explorers who sought riches there.

After the British and then the Dutch established settlements in what is today Suriname, economic growth opened the country to the outside world. Slaves and contract laborers were brought in from Africa, China, Java, and India, while more Europeans and people from the Middle East came to take advantage of the opportunities prosperity created. At the same time, native Indian tribes fled their coastal homelands, seeking refuge from the colonists. They resettled in the interior rain forest, where they were joined by escaped African slaves. The Dutch abolished slavery in 1863 and eventually granted internal control of the colony to its people.

Despite its weaknesses, Dutch rule gave the colony a stable government and good educational and health programs, and many of the immigrants who came to Dutch Guiana remained there. Creoles descended from African slaves emerged as the largest and most influential group in the country's multiethnic society. Javanese, Chinese, Europeans, and Middle Easterners also formed distinct ethnic populations, and the Hindus eventually rivaled the Creoles in numbers and influence.

No one knows how much longer the Surinamese interior will remain undeveloped.

These diverse societies coexisted in peace, yet conflict touched Suriname many times. European powers fought one another as well as the Indian and Maroon societies to maintain their prosperous colonies. And although almost 200 years of continuous Dutch rule created stability, many of the country's people called for self-government. Their movement succeeded in 1975, but soon after independence the era of peace ended. Several coup attempts threatened to topple Suriname's first government, and the administration finally fell to military forces after only five years in power. Even though Democratic government was restored by the early 1990s, Suriname's once-flourishing economy is still feeling the effects of the years of turmoil.

Yet much of the past remains. Today, Suriname's diverse ethnic groups for the most part live harmoniously together while preserving their own languages and cultural traditions in the face of modernization. The country's interior region remains remote and sparsely populated by Indians and Maroon people, who have adapted well to the harsh environment. Political leaders from these groups have emerged on the national scene, where their voices are being heard along with those of other groups. The future of Suriname will depend on the will and ability of all Surinamese to build their country on the basis of national unity.

◄ G L O S S A R Y ►

Amoksie Sranan for "mixture." It refers to the policy of blending different ethnic, racial, and religious groups into a harmonious and unified nation.

Batik A type of dyed cloth produced by the Javanese. It may feature abstract designs or pictures of people or places.

Bigi jari The "big year" celebrations for older people whose birthdays are a multiple of ten. These large parties are an important part of Creole family and social life.

Cassava A starchy plant whose root is the source of tapioca flour. It is a major food source in Suriname.

Creoles Descendants of black African slaves who live in Suriname's coastal region. The Creoles were strongly associated with the independence movement.

Er'eri A Creole dish of rice, bananas, breadfruit, codfish, and cassava.

Gamelan A Javanese percussion instrument.

Granman The chief of a Maroon village or settlement.

Kotomisi The traditional costume of Creole women, featuring many layers of petticoats topped by a long, full-skirted dress that is brightly colored. A starched cotton headscarf is tied in an intricate pattern of knots.

Lianas Vines that climb high into trees in the rain forest. Some varieties have brilliantly colored flowers.

Maroon societies Six ethnic groups descended from runaway slaves who escaped to the rain forest in past centuries. The

Maroon societies still inhabit the jungles of the interior.

Moksie metie A Chinese-style dish of cooked meat served over rice.

Obeah A charm of shells or grasses worn around the neck by Maroons who believe it will ward off evil spirits.

Pasa The name used by Surinamese Muslims for Ramadan, a month-long Islamic religious ceremony that involves fasting and daily attendance at a mosque.

Polder An area of land reclaimed from the sea by dikes and landfills. The Dutch mastered the use of polders in the Netherlands and brought the skill with them to Guiana.

Pom A Creole dish of chicken, tomatoes, lemon, and ground tajers.

Roti A Hindu dish consisting of a round, flat piece of bread wrapped around pieces of chicken and potato.

Rijsttafel Literally "rice table," an elaborate Javanese meal in which rice is accompanied by 15 or more side dishes of meat, fish, peppers, and other vegetables.

Satay A Javanese dish consisting of bits of pork or beef grilled on a stick and seasoned with a spicy sauce of peppers and peanuts.

Tajers Root vegetables used in Creole cooking.

Tandoor A clay oven used to bake many Hindu dishes, including roti.

Wayang Javanese for "play." Wayang performances usually feature puppets or actors wearing masks and a plot narrated by a storyteller.

◄ I N D E X ►

ACKNOWLEDGMENTS

The author and publisher are grateful to the following sources for photographs: ALCOA (pp. 16, 70, 75); AP/Wide World (p. 66); Library of Congress (pp. 26, 41, 82); Scott Mori/New York Botanical Gardens (pp. 52a, 56b); National Anthropological Archives (pp. 47, 60, 86); National Archives (pp. 36, 64, 78); National Zoo (p. 23); Organization of American States (pp. 29, 44, 45, 58, 85); Photo Researchers, Inc. (pp. 2, 14, 50a, 53, 54a, 55, 56a, 73, 80); G.T. Prance/New York Botanical Gardens (pp. 18, 24, 39, 50b, 51a, 52c, 59, 62, 72, 76, 88, 90); Smithsonian Institution (pp. 49, 54b); UPI/Bettmann Newsphotos (pp. 32, 34, 68); William Wayt Thomas (pp. 51b, 52b, 54–55). Photo Editor: Marty Baldessari. Photo Research: Joanne Stern.